THIS BOOK BELONGS
TO

_____

_____

_____

WRITTEN BY IZZY HOUSE
ILLUSTRATED BY MISS DEE DASSEN

Izzy and Dee Adventures -
The Moon Tree Companion Passport
Track and Celebrate Your Moon Tree Journey!

©Copyright 2025

AUTHOR – IZZY HOUSE
ILLUSTRATOR – MISS DEE DASSEN

FIRST EDITION

HARDCOVER ISBN: 979-8-9919343-8-1
PAPERBACK ISBN: 979-8-9919343-9-8

Moon trees, Moon trees, how tall will you grow?

Moon trees, Moon trees, where WILL YOU go?

BLAST OFF ON AN ADVENTURE TO FIND THE MOON TREES!

Izzy and Dee's parents bring home a tiny Moon tree—a baby tree from seeds that traveled to space! The sisters are excited to learn more, so they build a rocket out of cardboard and blast off on an exciting adventure.

They visit magical Moon trees all over the world, meeting new friends and discovering important lessons about being strong, working together, and dreaming big.

Unlike their imaginative story of their journey, you can visit the Moon Trees in reality and have keepsake of your visits with this Companion Passport.

Join Izzy and Dee to discover that anything is possible when you reach for the stars!

Each time you visit a Moon Tree, log it into this Moon Tree Companion Passport.

DISCLAIMER: TREES MAY NOT BE PRESENT AT ALL LISTED LOCATIONS DUE TO NATURAL CHANGES OR RELOCATIONS.

There is several pages for each of the six species of Moon Tree.

Draw a picture in the space, add a photo, write about your visit, and place a sticker for that location. *(Please leave the tree like you found it. Don't take its leaves, bark, or any of its parts.)*

You can get stickers and other stuff to commemorate your visit like backpacks, pillow, wall clocks, and more to decorate your room at -

MissDeeDassen.com
(Please contact us if you don't see your location)

APOLLO MOON TREES

There was a brave astronaut named Stuart Roosa, who dreamed of reaching the stars. Before he flew to space, Stuart had an exciting job leaping out of airplanes as a smoke-jumper, helping to fight forest fires deep in the woods. His love for trees and adventure made him the perfect person to partner with the U.S. Forest Service to carry a very special treasure on the Apollo 14 mission—tiny tree seeds!

In 1971, Stuart's job was to fly the spaceship Kitty Hawk around the Moon while his friends, Alan and Edgar, explored the lunar surface. High above the Moon, Stuart and his seeds floated in space, dancing weightlessly among the stars.

When he returned to Earth, those seeds grew into beautiful "Moon Trees," living reminders of Stuart's amazing journey and how space can impact our Earth!

These Moon trees were planted all around the world. The trees faded into memory as they grew. One day, Dr. David R. Williams from NASA set about to find all of the locations of these inspirational trees and discover how well they grew.

Where are the Apollo Moon Trees?

You can find a list of Moon Trees on the NASA Moon Tree website, which provides an updated map and information about their locations. If you know of one that is not listed, please contact them.

Visit **nssdc.gsfc.NASA.gov/planetary/lunar/moon_tree.html** to explore their status, history and placement.

DISCLAIMER: TREES MAY NOT BE PRESENT AT ALL LISTED LOCATIONS DUE TO NATURAL CHANGES OR RELOCATIONS.

(If you know of an Apollo Moon Tree that is not on the list or has changed status, be sure to tell Dr. David Williams and he will get it listed. His contact information is on the website.)

What kind of species are the
Apollo 14 Mission Moon Trees?

The Apollo 14 mission in 1971 carried seeds from five tree species:

- Loblolly Pine (*Pinus taeda*)
- Sycamore (*Platanus occidentalis*)
- Sweetgum (*Liquidambar styraciflua*)
- Redwood (*Sequoia sempervirens*)
- Douglas fir (*Pseudotsuga menziesii*)

ARTEMIS MOON TREES

The Artemis I Mission, launched in 2022, marked a major milestone in NASA's effort to return humans to the Moon. As an uncrewed test flight, it demonstrated the capabilities of the Space Launch System (SLS)—one of the most powerful rocket ever built—and the Orion spacecraft. The mission's goal was to test the spacecraft's systems in deep space, ensuring its readiness to safely carry astronauts on future missions. Artemis I successfully traveled over 1.4 million miles, circumnavigating the Moon before returning to Earth, paving the way for Artemis II, which will carry a crew.

The U.S. Forest Service plays a crucial role in the Artemis Moon Tree project by germinating and cultivating the Moon Tree seeds that were carried on the Artemis I mission. Drawing on its forestry expertise and a historical connection to the original Apollo 14 Moon Trees, the Forest Service ensures the successful growth of these seedlings.

In collaboration with NASA, the Forest Service oversees their distribution to schools, museums, universities, and science centers, promoting educational outreach and community engagement. This initiative highlights the connection between space exploration and environmental stewardship, using the Moon Trees as a living symbol to inspire interest in STEM fields and emphasize the importance of conservation.

Artemis 1 Mission Moon Trees Species

The Artemis mission carried seeds from five tree species:

- Loblolly Pine (*Pinus taeda*)
- American Sycamore: (*Platanus occidentalis*)
- Sweetgum (*Liquidambar styraciflua*)
- Giant Sequoias (*Sequoiadendron giganteum*)
- *Douglas Fir (Pseudotsuga menziesii)*

Where are the Artemis 1 Moon Trees?

Find the closest Artemis Moon Tree on this webpage -

NASA.gov/learning-resources/artemis-i-moon-tree-stewards

Would you like to plant an Artemis 1 Moon Tree?

Schools, museums, science centers, universities, and community organizations were invited to apply for a seedling through NASA's Artifact Module. Visit NASA's website to learn more.

NASA.gov/learning-resources/nasa-stem-artemis-moon-trees

You may not have a Moon Tree but you can learn how to grow a tree.

Growing a Moon Tree:

Forest Service (U.S. Department of Agriculture)
www.fs.usda.gov/learn/conservation-education/moon-trees

Moon Tree Information for Applicants: Planting and Care (and a great resource to grow non-Moon trees, too!)

www.fs.usda.gov/sites/default/files/fs_media/fs_document/Moon-Tree-Applicant-Information.pdf

More Moon Trees Educational Resources -
www.naturalinquirer.org/Artemis-Moon-Trees-v-397.html

SYCAMORE MOON TREE

About Sycamore trees

The sycamore tree is a majestic and towering giant, capable of reaching heights over 100 feet. Found in many parts of the United States, it is a common sight in parks, forests, and along waterways. One of its most distinctive features is its bark, which peels away in irregular patches, revealing a striking mosaic of white, gray, and brown underneath. This unique characteristic gives the tree an almost camouflage-like appearance.

Sycamore leaves are large and broad, shaped like stars with three to five pointed lobes, providing ample shade in the summer months. In the fall, the leaves turn golden brown before drifting to the ground. Another fascinating feature of the sycamore is its seed balls—small, round clusters that dangle from its branches and eventually fall during the winter. These seed balls often break apart, releasing fluffy seeds carried away by the wind or water.

Sycamores thrive in moist, fertile soils and are frequently found near rivers and streams. Their extensive root systems help stabilize the soil, preventing erosion and protecting the environment.

Sycamore trees are admired for their strength, resilience, and timeless beauty, making them a beloved symbol of nature's endurance and grace.

LIST OF KNOWN APOLLO MOON TREES - Sycamore:

Visit **nssdc.gsfc.nasa.gov/planetary/lunar/moon_tree.html** to explore their history and placement.

DISCLAIMER: TREES MAY NOT BE PRESENT AT ALL LISTED LOCATIONS DUE TO NATURAL CHANGES OR RELOCATIONS.

- **Birmingham Botanical Gardens** - Burmingham, Alabama
- **Botanical Gardens** - Asheville, North Carolina
- **Cambria County Courthouse** - Ebensburg, Pennsylvania
- **Camp Iti Kana** - Wiggins, Mississippi
- **Camp Koch Girl Scout Camp** - Cannelton, Indiana
- **Cascades Park** - Tallahassee, Florida
- **Core Creek Park** - Newtown/Langhorne, Pennsylvania
- **Coudersport Area Recreational Park** - Coudersport, Pennsylvania
- **Cradle of Forestry** - Pisgah National Forest, North Carolina
- **Dillsburg Elementary School** - Dillsburg, Pennsylvania
- **Fernwood Botanical Gardens** - Niles, Michigan
- **Friendship Park** - Jefferson County, Ohio
- **Goddard Space Flight Center** - Greenbelt, Maryland
- **Gough Park** - Silver City, New Mexico
- **Haywood Community College** - Clyde, North Carolina
- **Highland Hall** - Hollidaysburg, Pennsylvania
- **Holliston Police Station** - Holliston, Massachusetts
- **Indiana Statehouse** - Indianapolis, Indiana
- **International Forest of Friendship** - Atchison, Kansas
- **Keystone Heights Library** - Keystone Heights, Florida
- **Kings Dominion Amusement Park** - Doswell, Virginia
- **Lincoln State Park** - Lincoln City, Indiana
- **Lockheed Martin** - King of Prussia, Pennsylvania
- **Lone Peak Conservation Center** - Draper, Utah
- **Mississippi State University** - Starkville, Mississippi
- **Patrick Elementary School** - Hampton, Virginia
- **Private Residence** - Biloxi, Mississippi
- **Private Residence** - Westlake, Texas
- **River Ridge Campground** - Bracey, Virginia
- **Topton Mini Museum** - Topton, Pennsylvania
- **University of Arizona** - Tucson, Arizona
- **University of Florida** - Gainesville, Florida
- **University of the South** - Sewanee, Tennessee
- **Walther Park** - DeSoto, Missouri
- **Chateau Lafayette** - Chavaniac, France

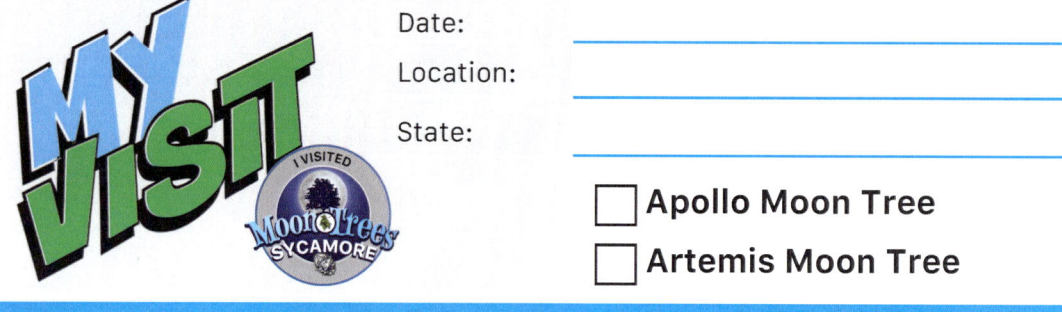

Date: _____

Location: _____

State: _____

☐ **Apollo Moon Tree**
☐ **Artemis Moon Tree**

FUN FACTS

○
○
○
○
○
○
○
○

"With its peeling bark, the sycamore shows us that letting go of the old makes way for something new."

I AM INSPIRED BY...

MORE STUFF:

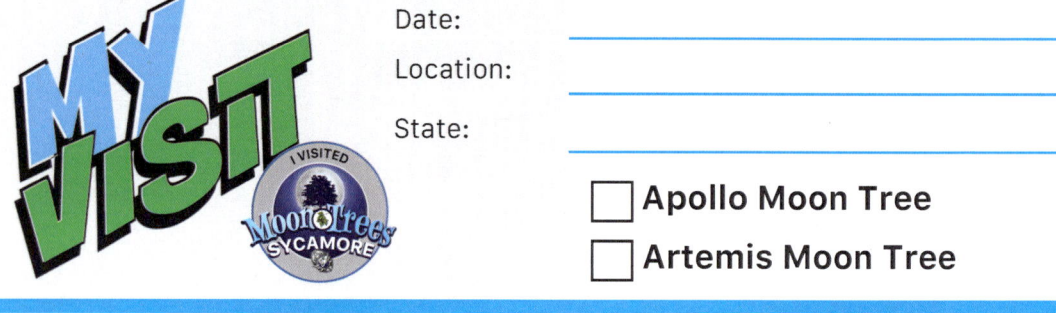

Date: _____

Location: _____

State: _____

☐ **Apollo Moon Tree**

☐ **Artemis Moon Tree**

FUN FACTS

○

○

○

○

○

○

○

○

"The sycamore reminds us that true strength isn't about being unshaken—it's about standing tall regardless of what comes your way."

I AM INSPIRED BY...

MORE STUFF:

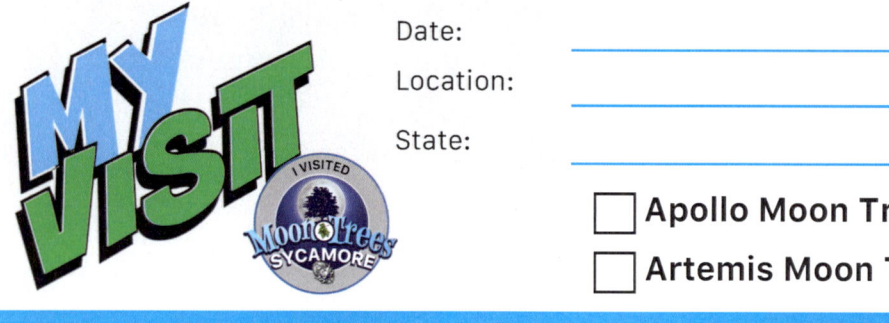

Date: _____

Location: _____

State: _____

☐ Apollo Moon Tree
☐ Artemis Moon Tree

FUN FACTS

○
○
○
○
○
○
○
○

"The sycamore tree teaches us that true grace lies in growing steadily, adapting beautifully, and standing tall through all seasons."

I AM INSPIRED BY...

MORE STUFF:

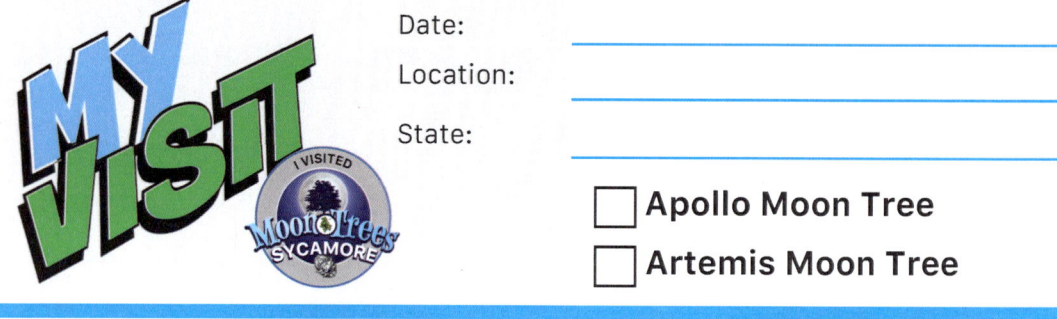

Date: _____

Location: _____

State: _____

☐ **Apollo Moon Tree**
☐ **Artemis Moon Tree**

FUN FACTS

○
○
○
○
○
○
○
○

"The sycamore tree reminds us that real strength comes from deep roots and the courage to grow tall, despite challenges."

I AM INSPIRED BY...

MORE STUFF:

About a Loblolly Pine

The loblolly pine (Pinus taeda) is a fast-growing and versatile evergreen tree native to the southeastern United States. Often reaching heights of 60–100 feet, it is one of the most common and commercially significant pine species in the region. It is used for lumber, paper, wood products, reforestation and carbon sequetration, and bioenergy.

Its tall, straight trunk is covered in thick, reddish-brown bark with deep ridges, giving it a distinctive textured appearance.

Its long, slender needles, which grow in bundles of three, range from 6 to 10 inches and provide a lush, green canopy year-round. The loblolly pine produces oval-shaped cones about 3–6 inches long, which house its seeds.

It thrives in a variety of habitats, including lowland areas, wetlands, and sandy soils, but is especially abundant in floodplains and areas with moist, acidic soils.

Symbolically, the loblolly pine represents resilience, strength, and adaptability, reflecting its ability to flourish in diverse environments. It is also a symbol of growth and renewal, as it is widely used in reforestation projects. Known for its beauty and ecological importance, the loblolly pine provides habitats for wildlife, preventing erosion, and serving as a key resource for the timber industry.

LIST OF KNOWN APOLLO MOON TREES - Loblolly:

Visit **nssdc.gsfc.nasa.gov/planetary/lunar/moon_tree.html** to explore their history and placement.

DISCLAIMER: TREES MAY NOT BE PRESENT AT ALL LISTED LOCATIONS DUE TO NATURAL CHANGES OR RELOCATIONS.

Clarke County Planning Dept. - Athens, Georgia
Doyle Conner Building - Tallahassee, Florida
Forest Capital State Park - Perry, Florida
Georgia Forestry Center - Macon, Georgia
Ivy Green - Tuscumbia, Alabama
Lowell Elementary School - Boise, Idaho
Okefenokee RESA - Waycross, Georgia
Old Washington Historic State Park - Washington, Arkansas
Palustris Experimental Forest - Elmer, Louisiana
Pioneer Museum of Alabama - Troy,Alabama
Sebastian County Courthouse - Ft. Smith, Arkansas
Society of American Foresters - Bethesda, Maryland
Montgomery State Capitol - Montgomery, Alabama
University of Tennessee - Knoxville, Tennessee
VA Medical Center - Tuskegee, Alabama

ARTEMIS MOON TREES

Visit **nasa.gov/learning-resources/artemis-i-moon-tree-stewards/** for a list of the Artemis Moon Trees. This list is changing as new trees are planted.

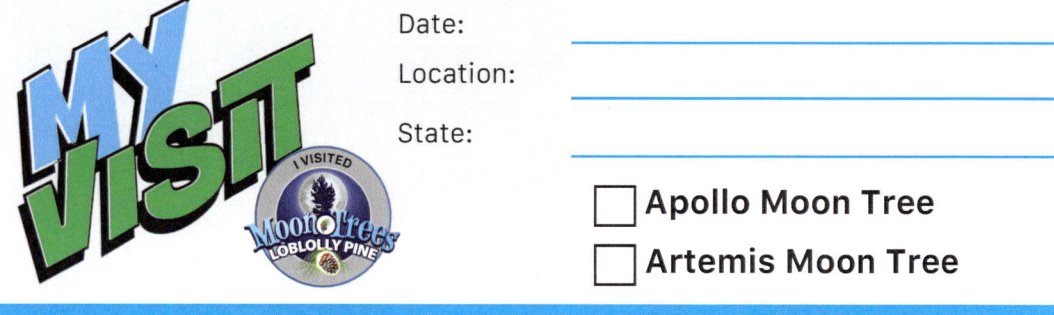

Date: _____

Location: _____

State: _____

☐ **Apollo Moon Tree**
☐ **Artemis Moon Tree**

FUN FACTS

○
○
○
○
○
○
○
○

"Stand tall and reach for the sky, just like the loblolly pine—your roots keep you grounded, but your dreams can enable you to soar to great heights!"

I AM INSPIRED BY...

MORE STUFF:

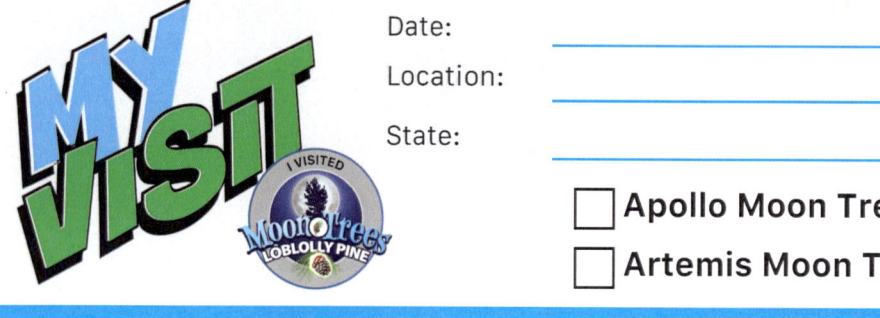

Date: _____

Location: _____

State: _____

☐ Apollo Moon Tree
☐ Artemis Moon Tree

FUN FACTS

○
○
○
○
○
○
○
○

"The loblolly pine shows us that success comes from finding a way to grow, even in unexpected conditions."

I AM INSPIRED BY...

MORE STUFF:

Date: _____

Location: _____

State: _____

☐ Apollo Moon Tree
☐ Artemis Moon Tree

FUN FACTS

○
○
○
○
○
○
○
○

*"The loblolly pine grows in many places because it adapts—
just like you can adjust and thrive anywhere life takes you."*

I AM INSPIRED BY...

MORE STUFF:

Date: _____

Location: _____

State: _____

☐ Apollo Moon Tree
☐ Artemis Moon Tree

FUN FACTS

○
○
○
○
○
○
○
○

"The Loblolly Pine Moon Tree stands as a living testament to resilience and exploration—rooted in the Earth yet touched by the stars. It reminds us that growth knows no boundaries, whether on this planet or beyond."

I AM INSPIRED BY...

MORE STUFF:

SWEETGUM MOON TREE

About SweetGum trees

The sweetgum tree (Liquidambar styraciflua) is a tall, deciduous tree known for its vibrant fall colors and distinctive star-shaped leaves. Growing up to 100 feet tall, the sweetgum has a straight trunk with deeply ridged gray-brown bark and a broad, rounded canopy.

Its glossy green leaves, shaped like five-pointed stars, turn stunning shades of red, orange, yellow, and purple in the fall, creating a spectacular display of autumn beauty.

Sweetgum trees produce unique, spiky, ball-shaped seed pods, often called "gumballs," which hang from the branches and fall to the ground in winter.

Native to the southeastern United States and parts of Central America, including Mexico, Belize, El Salvador, Honduras, and Nicaragua, these trees thrive in a variety of habitats, from bottomlands and riverbanks to urban areas, due to their adaptability and tolerance to different soil types.

The Sweetgum tree has been successfully cultivated in several other countries and regions due to its ornamental value and adaptability including Europe, Asia, Australia, New Zealand, and South America.

Symbolically, the sweetgum tree represents balance, renewal, and transformation. Its brilliant fall colors remind us of the beauty in change, while its strong, straight growth reflects resilience and endurance.

A beloved part of the landscape, the sweetgum tree inspires awe and serves as a symbol of nature's enduring cycle of growth and renewal.

LIST OF KNOWN APOLLO MOON TREES - Sweetgum:

Visit *nssdc.gsfc.nasa.gov/planetary/lunar/moon_tree.html* to explore their history and placement.

DISCLAIMER: TREES MAY NOT BE PRESENT AT ALL LISTED LOCATIONS DUE TO NATURAL CHANGES OR RELOCATIONS.

Loudoun County, Virginia - Scott Jenkins Memorial Park
Brasilia, Brazil - IBAMA Institute

ARTEMIS MOON TREES

Visit *nasa.gov/learning-resources/artemis-i-moon-tree-stewards/* for a list of the Artemis Moon Trees. This list is changing as new trees are planted.

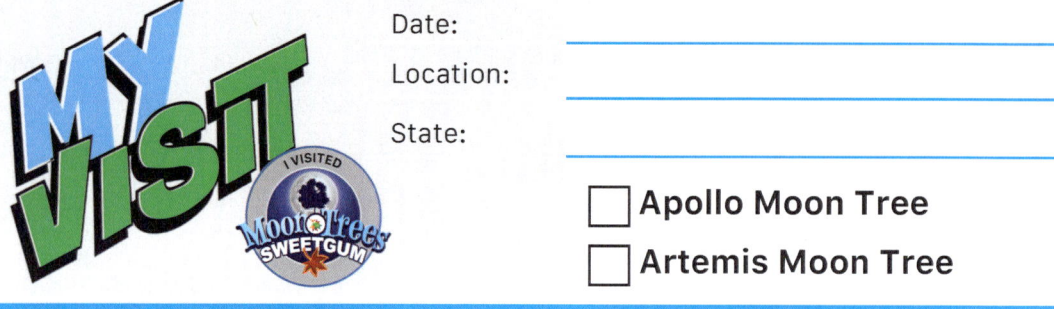

Date: _____

Location: _____

State: _____

☐ **Apollo Moon Tree**
☐ **Artemis Moon Tree**

FUN FACTS

○
○
○
○
○
○
○
○

"The sweetgum tree shows us that change can be beautiful, just like its leaves turning bright colors in the fall."

I AM INSPIRED BY...

MORE STUFF:

Date: _____

Location: _____

State: _____

☐ **Apollo Moon Tree**
☐ **Artemis Moon Tree**

FUN FACTS

○
○
○
○
○
○
○
○

"Just like the stars in the sky, the sweetgum's leaves shine brightly, showing us the beauty in standing out."

I AM INSPIRED BY...

MORE STUFF:

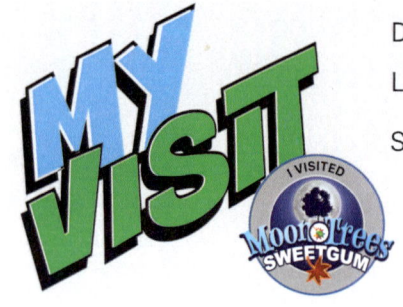

Date: _____

Location: _____

State: _____

☐ **Apollo Moon Tree**
☐ **Artemis Moon Tree**

FUN FACTS

○
○
○
○
○
○
○
○

"Just like the sweetgum tree, we grow and change with each season, becoming stronger and brighter along the way."

I AM INSPIRED BY...

MORE STUFF:

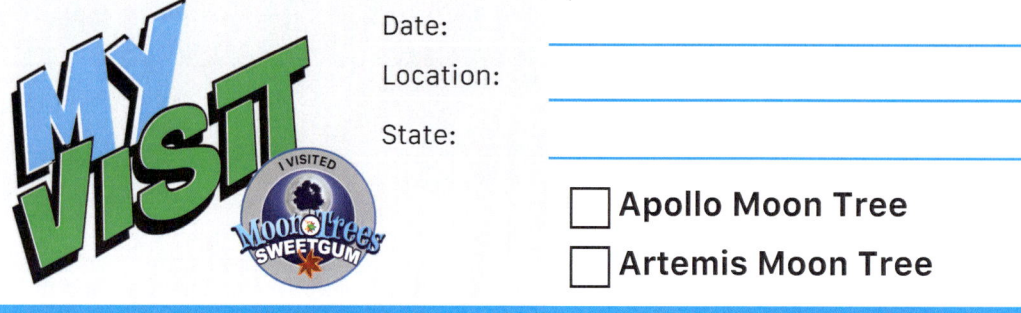

Date: _____

Location: _____

State: _____

☐ **Apollo Moon Tree**

☐ **Artemis Moon Tree**

FUN FACTS

○

○

○

○

○

○

○

○

"The sweetgum tree shows us that transformation is beautiful— its leaves change colors to create something magical."

I AM INSPIRED BY...

MORE STUFF:

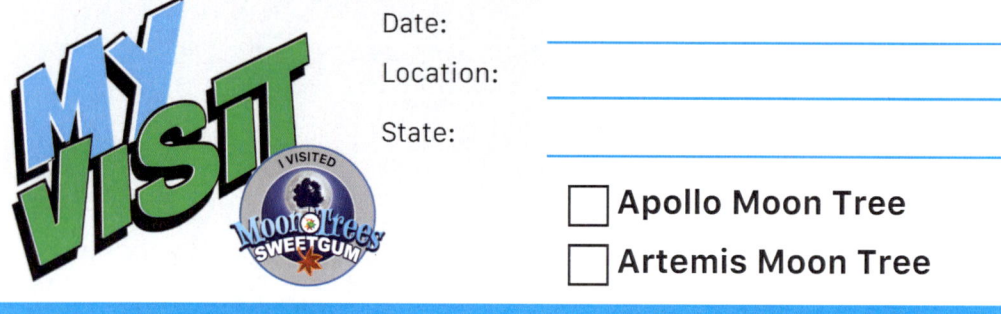

Date: _____

Location: _____

State: _____

☐ **Apollo Moon Tree**
☐ **Artemis Moon Tree**

FUN FACTS

○
○
○
○
○
○
○
○

"The Sweetgum Moon Tree embodies transformation and renewal, with its vibrant leaves and celestial journey reminding us that growth is a beautiful process rooted in resilience and wonder."

I AM INSPIRED BY...

MORE STUFF:

REDWOOD MOON TREE

About a Redwoods

The redwood (Sequoia sempervirens) is one of the most awe-inspiring trees on Earth, known for its incredible height and longevity. These towering evergreens can reach heights of over 300 feet, with trunks that span up to 20 feet in diameter. Redwoods are some of the tallest trees in the world, with a lifespan that can exceed 2,000 years. Their reddish-brown bark, thick and spongy, provides protection against fire and pests, contributing to their remarkable endurance.

The redwood's leaves are flat, needle-like, and deep green, arranged in a feathery pattern along slender branches. These leaves play a crucial role in the tree's ability to capture moisture from the foggy coastal air where redwoods typically thrive. Native to the coastal regions of northern California and southern Oregon, redwoods grow in cool, moist climates with frequent fog, which helps sustain their immense size. Symbolically, the redwood represents

resilience, longevity, and connection. These trees have withstood centuries of natural challenges, serving as a reminder of nature's strength and persistence.

Their vast height and interconnected root systems also symbolize community and support, as redwoods rely on one another for stability.

Revered for their majesty and ecological importance, redwoods inspire awe, reminding us of the beauty and power of the natural world.

LIST OF KNOWN APOLLO MOON TREES - Redwood:

Visit **nssdc.gsfc.nasa.gov/planetary/lunar/moon_tree.html** to explore their history and placement.

DISCLAIMER: TREES MAY NOT BE PRESENT AT ALL LISTED LOCATIONS DUE TO NATURAL CHANGES OR RELOCATIONS.

Berkeley, California - Tilden Nature Area
Arcata, California - Humboldt State University
Lockeford, California - Lockeford Plant Materials Center
Monterey, California - Friendly Plaza
Sacramento, California - Capitol Park
San Luis Obispo, California - Mission Plaza
Cambara do Sul, Brazil - Praça Central São José
Rio Grande do Sul, Brazil - Santa Rosa

ARTEMIS MOON TREES

Visit **nasa.gov/learning-resources/artemis-i-moon-tree-stewards/** for a list of the Artemis Moon Trees. This list is changing as new trees are planted.

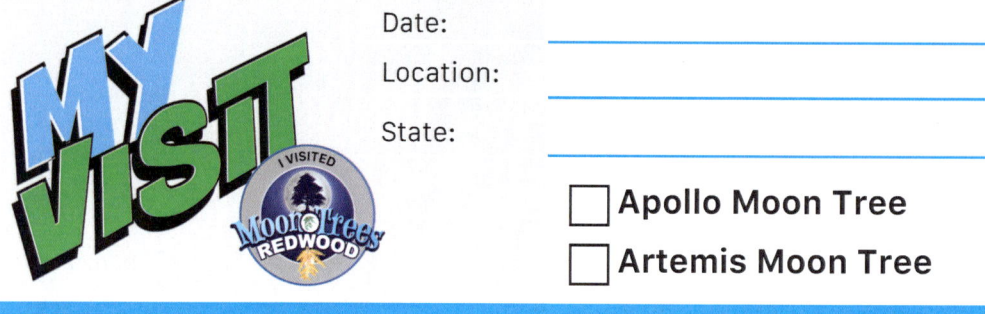

Date: _____

Location: _____

State: _____

☐ Apollo Moon Tree
☐ Artemis Moon Tree

FUN FACTS

- ○
- ○
- ○
- ○
- ○
- ○
- ○
- ○

"Even the mightiest redwood relies on its neighbors—teamwork makes the tallest dreams possible."

I AM INSPIRED BY...

MORE STUFF:

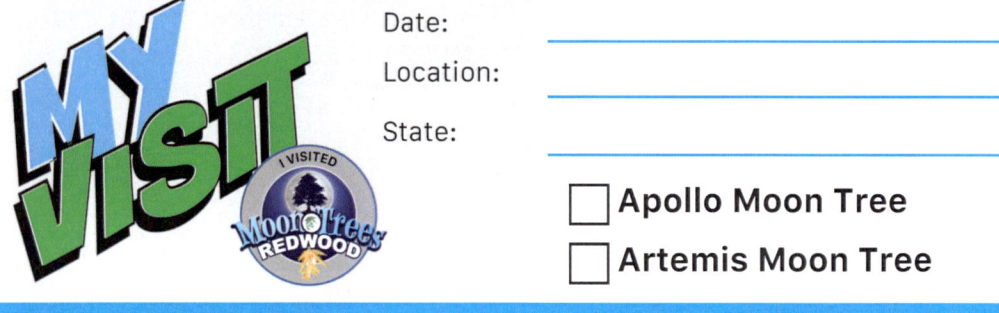

Date: _____

Location: _____

State: _____

☐ Apollo Moon Tree

☐ Artemis Moon Tree

FUN FACTS

○
○
○
○
○
○
○
○

"Redwoods remind us that connections make us tall—every friendship helps us grow."

I AM INSPIRED BY...

MORE STUFF:

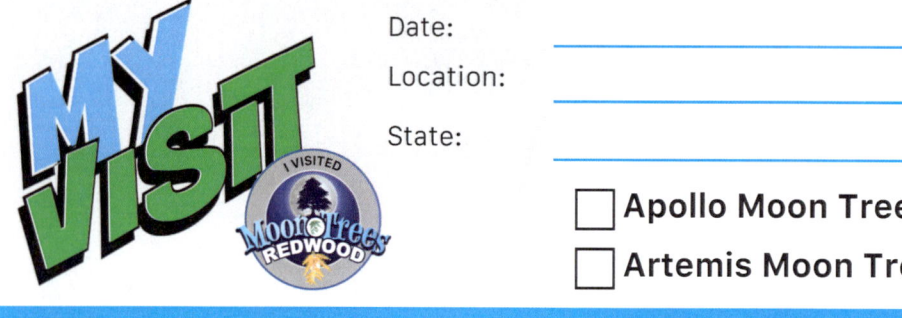

Date: _____

Location: _____

State: _____

☐ **Apollo Moon Tree**

☐ **Artemis Moon Tree**

FUN FACTS

○

○

○

○

○

○

○

○

"The redwood shows us that resilience is not just about surviving, but thriving through every test of time."

I AM INSPIRED BY...

MORE STUFF:

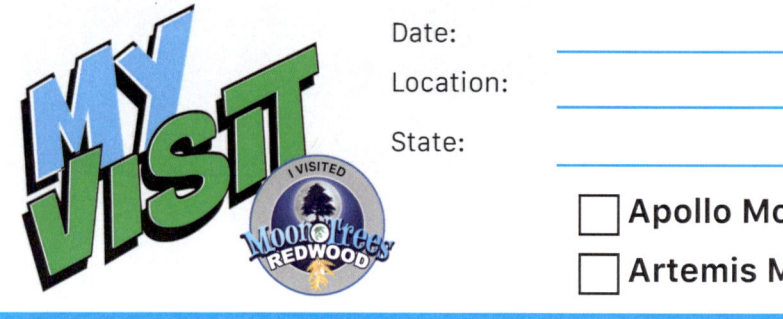

Date: _____

Location: _____

State: _____

☐ **Apollo Moon Tree**
☐ **Artemis Moon Tree**

FUN FACTS

○
○
○
○
○
○
○
○

"The redwood teaches us that great heights are possible with patience and determination."

I AM INSPIRED BY...

MORE STUFF:

DOUGLAS FIR MOON TREE

About Dougls Fir Trees

The Douglas fir (Pseudotsuga menziesii) is a majestic evergreen tree known for its towering height, soft needles, and importance in forests and human use. These trees can grow over 300 feet tall in ideal conditions, with straight trunks and a pyramidal shape that makes them a classic symbol of coniferous forests. The bark of a mature Douglas fir is thick, reddish-brown, and deeply grooved, offering protection against fire and pests.

The tree's soft, flat needles are dark green with a subtle bluish hue and grow spirally along its branches. When crushed, the needles release a pleasant, citrus-like aroma. Its cones are oval-shaped and distinctive, with unique, three-pointed bracts that resemble tiny mouse tails peeking out from under the cone scales.

Douglas fir trees are native to western North America, thriving in diverse environments from coastal rainforests to the Rocky Mountains. They are commonly found in Oregon, Washington, California, and British Columbia and are highly adaptable to various elevations and soil types.

Symbolically, the Douglas fir represents resilience, protection, and renewal. Its strength and longevity make it a symbol of endurance, while its towering presence inspires awe and respect for nature.

Additionally, the Douglas fir is often associated with celebration and connection, as it is widely used as a Christmas tree, bringing people together during the holidays.

This versatile and iconic tree is a testament to the beauty, strength, and interconnectedness of the natural world.

LIST OF KNOWN APOLLO MOON TREES - Douglas Fir:

Visit **nssdc.gsfc.nasa.gov/planetary/lunar/moon_tree.html** to explore their history and placement.

DISCLAIMER: TREES MAY NOT BE PRESENT AT ALL LISTED LOCATIONS DUE TO NATURAL CHANGES OR RELOCATIONS.

Santa Fe, New Mexico - State Capitol Building
Corvallis, Oregon - Oregon State University
Eugene, Oregon - University of Oregon
Roseburg, Oregon - U.S. Veteran's Hospital
Salem, Oregon - State Capitol Building
Olympia, Washington - State Capitol Building

ARTEMIS MOON TREES

Visit **nasa.gov/learning-resources/artemis-i-moon-tree-stewards/** for a list of the Artemis Moon Trees. This list is changing as new trees are planted.

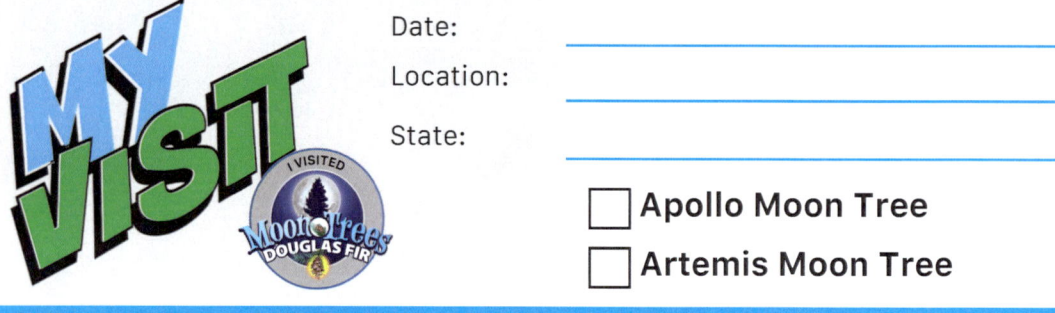

Date: _____

Location: _____

State: _____

☐ **Apollo Moon Tree**
☐ **Artemis Moon Tree**

FUN FACTS

○
○
○
○
○
○
○
○

*"The Douglas fir reminds us to honor nature,
where every tree, leaf, and root plays a part in creating
the world's beauty and balance."*

I AM INSPIRED BY...

MORE STUFF:

Date: _____

Location: _____

State: _____

☐ **Apollo Moon Tree**
☐ **Artemis Moon Tree**

FUN FACTS

○
○
○
○
○
○
○
○

"With its evergreen needles, the Douglas fir shows us that we can stay bright and steady through all seasons."

I AM INSPIRED BY...

MORE STUFF:

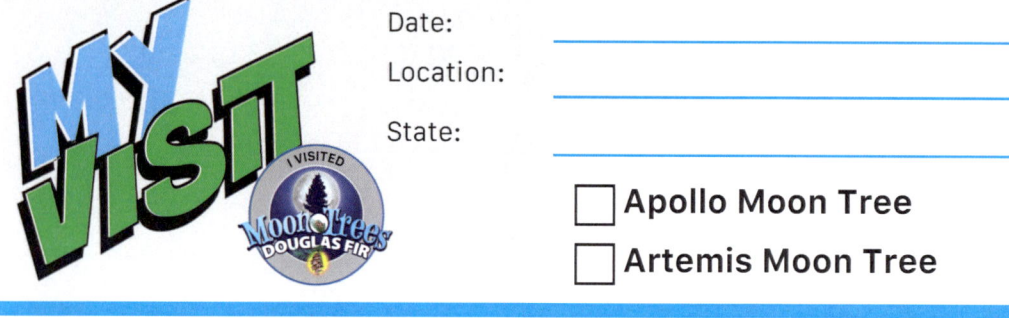

Date: _____

Location: _____

State: _____

☐ Apollo Moon Tree
☐ Artemis Moon Tree

FUN FACTS

○
○
○
○
○
○
○
○

"The Douglas fir teaches us that interconnectedness is the key to strength—its roots support the forest, just as we support each other."

I AM INSPIRED BY...

MORE STUFF:

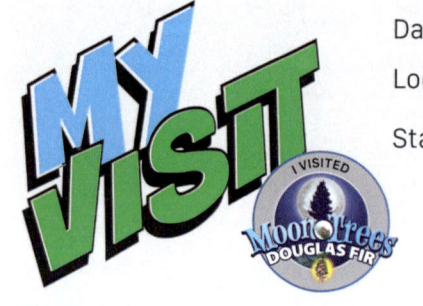

Date: _____

Location: _____

State: _____

☐ Apollo Moon Tree
☐ Artemis Moon Tree

FUN FACTS

○
○
○
○
○
○
○
○

*"The Douglas fir stands tall and strong.
Its canopy of branches remind us that
true protection comes from offering shelter
and support to those around us."*

I AM INSPIRED BY...

MORE STUFF:

GIANT SEQUOIA MOON TREE

About Giant Sequoia Trees

The giant sequoia (Sequoiadendron giganteum) is one of the most awe-inspiring trees on Earth, known for its incredible size, age, and resilience. These ancient giants can grow over 250 feet tall, with trunks reaching diameters of up to 30 feet, making them the largest trees in the world by volume. Their reddish-brown bark is thick, spongy, and fire-resistant, contributing to their remarkable ability to survive harsh conditions and thrive for thousands of years.

The tree's evergreen leaves are small, scale-like, and tightly arranged along the branches, creating a dense, lush canopy that remains vibrant year-round. Giant sequoias produce cones that are 2–3 inches long, which can release seeds when exposed to heat or fire, a natural process that helps these trees regenerate and maintain their ecosystems.

Giant sequoias are native to the western slopes of California's Sierra Nevada mountains, where they grow in small, scattered groves at elevations between 4,000 and 8,000 feet.

They thrive in well-drained soils and rely on the region's winter snowpack for moisture.

Symbolically, the giant sequoia represents strength, longevity, and resilience. These trees serve as living monuments to the passage of time, often surviving for more than 3,000 years.

Their towering presence and enduring nature inspire awe and remind us of the importance of conservation and the interconnectedness of life on Earth.

Revered as symbols of endurance and grandeur, giant sequoias are a testament to the wonders of the natural world.

ARTEMIS MOON TREES

The Artemis I mission included Giant Sequoia seeds instead of the coast redwood seeds flown during Apollo 14.

Visit *nasa.gov/learning-resources/artemis-i-moon-tree-stewards/* for a list of the Artemis Moon Trees. This list is changing as new trees are planted.

DISCLAIMER: TREES MAY NOT BE PRESENT AT ALL LISTED LOCATIONS DUE TO NATURAL CHANGES OR RELOCATIONS.

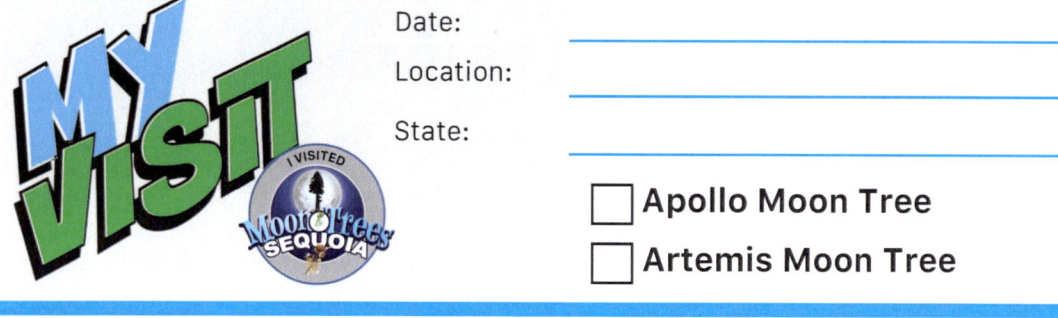

Date: _____

Location: _____

State: _____

☐ Apollo Moon Tree
☐ Artemis Moon Tree

FUN FACTS

○
○
○
○
○
○
○
○

"Standing before a giant sequoia fills us with awe and wonder, reminding us of the incredible beauty nature can create."

I AM INSPIRED BY...

MORE STUFF:

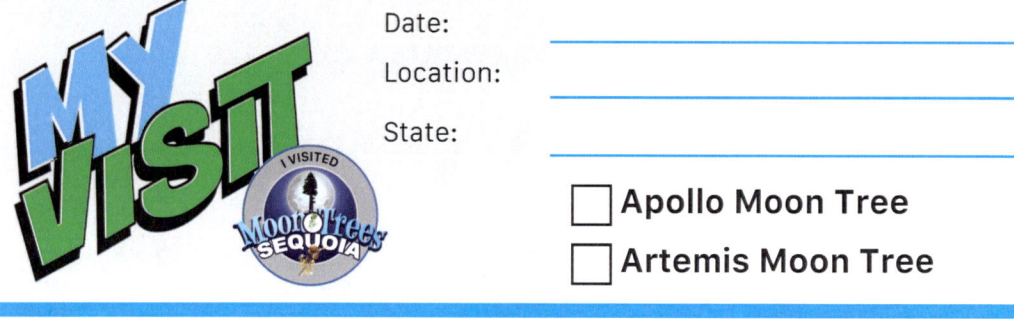

Date: _____

Location: _____

State: _____

☐ **Apollo Moon Tree**
☐ **Artemis Moon Tree**

FUN FACTS

○
○
○
○
○
○
○
○

*"The giant sequoia shows us that thinking big starts small—
every towering tree began with a tiny seed,
nurtured by patience, care, and the belief that
greatness takes time to grow."*

I AM INSPIRED BY...

MORE STUFF:

Date:

Location:

State:

☐ **Apollo Moon Tree**
☐ **Artemis Moon Tree**

FUN FACTS

○
○
○
○
○
○
○
○

*"Protecting the giant sequoia is more than saving a tree—
it's preserving a legacy of strength, resilience,
and the beauty of nature for future generations."*

I AM INSPIRED BY...

MORE STUFF:

Date: _____

Location: _____

State: _____

☐ Apollo Moon Tree
☐ Artemis Moon Tree

FUN FACTS

○
○
○
○
○
○
○
○

"The giant sequoia shows us that interconnectedness is the key to strength— its roots link with others to support its towering presence."

I AM INSPIRED BY...

MORE STUFF:

Join Izzy and Dee on extraordinary adventures as they uncover the wonders of science, engineering, our world, and the vast universe beyond! Subscribe now to be the first to know about their next exciting launch.

www.ingramcontent.com/pod-product-compliance
Lightning Source LLC
Chambersburg PA
CBRC090839120626
46551CB00008B/699